FOOD LOVERS

CAKES & BAKES

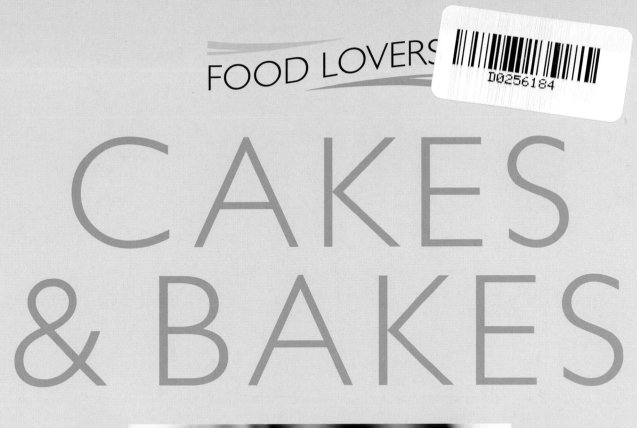

RECIPES SELECTED BY JONNIE LÉGER

Trans
Atlantic
Press

CONTENTS

BLACKBERRY SLICES

Ingredients

1¹/₃ cups/300 g butter

8 eggs

1 cup/200 g sugar

2 tsp. vanilla extract

Grated zest of ½ unwaxed lemon

1¼ cups/125 g all-purpose (plain) flour

1½ cups/300 g cream of wheat (semolina)

1½ tsp. baking powder

3 cups/400 g blackberries

Confectioners' (icing) sugar, for dusting

Ground pistachios, for sprinkling

Method

Prep and cook time 1 hour

1 Preheat the oven to 180°C/350°F/Gas Mark 4. Line a shallow baking pan (tin), measuring about 15 x 10 inch / 38 x 25 cm, with baking parchment.

2 Beat the butter until light and fluffy. Separate 6 of the eggs. Gradually beat the egg yolks and the remaining 2 whole eggs into the butter with ¾ cup/150 g of the sugar, the vanilla extract and grated lemon zest, alternating the addition of the eggs with the other ingredients.

3 Mix the flour, cream of wheat (semolina) and baking powder together and gradually stir into the egg mixture.

4 Whisk the egg whites until stiff, gradually trickling in the remaining sugar. Carefully fold into the batter with the blackberries. Spread the batter in the prepared baking pan.

5 Bake in the oven for 35-40 minutes. Leave to cool and then dust with confectioners' (icing) sugar and sprinkle with ground pistachios. Cut into rectangles to serve.

Makes about 16

SCOTTISH DUNDEE CAKE

Ingredients

1–1¼ cup/180 g golden raisins (sultanas)

¾ cup/125 g finely chopped figs

1–1¼ cup/180 g currants

Grated zest of 1 lemon

3 tbsp. whiskey

6–8 candied cherries, quartered

¹/₃ cup/50 g candied lemon peel, finely chopped

¹/₃ cup/50 g candied orange peel, finely chopped

2½ cups/250 g all-purpose (plain) flour

1½ tsp. baking powder

¾ cup/180 g butter

²/₃ cup/125 g sugar

1 tbsp. honey

3 large eggs

¹/₃ cup/75 ml milk

Blanched almonds, for decorating

Confectioners' (icing sugar) for dusting

Marzipan (optional), for covering

Method

Prep and cook time 2 hours 30 min.

1 Preheat the oven to 180°C/350°F/Gas Mark 4. Grease and line a 10 inch/26 cm spring-release cake pan (tin).

2 Mix the raisins (sultanas), figs and currants with the lemon zest, whiskey and candied fruits in a large bowl and leave to stand.

3 Meanwhile, sift the flour and baking powder together. Cream the butter with the sugar and honey until light and fluffy. Gradually beat in the eggs and then beat in the flour, milk and soaked dried fruit. Turn the batter into the prepared cake pan and smooth the top. Decorate the top of the cake with the whole almonds.

4 Bake in the oven for 30 minutes, then reduce the oven temperature to 150°C/300°F/Gas Mark 2 and bake for a further 90 minutes. Cover the top with baking parchment if it browns too quickly. Cool in the pan for 15 minutes then take out and leave to cool completely.

5 Before serving, dust with confectioners' (icing) sugar and cover the sides of the cake with marzipan if wished.

Serves about 12

SPICED RAISIN CAKE

Ingredients

²/₃ cup/150 g butter, plus extra for greasing

2 tbsp. cocoa powder, plus extra for dusting

8 eggs

½ cup/100 g sugar

2½ cups/250 g all-purpose (plain) flour

1¹/₃ cups/200 g raisins

1 tbsp. cinnamon

Large pinch ground cloves

²/₃ cup/150 ml whipping cream

1 tsp. vanilla extract

Ground cinnamon

Method

Prep and cook time: 1 hour 25 min.

1 Preheat the oven to 180°C/350°F/Gas Mark 4. Butter a 12 x 4½ inch/30 x 11.5 cm loaf pan (tin) and dust with cocoa powder.

2 Melt the butter and leave to cool slightly. Separate the eggs. Add the sugar to the egg yolks and beat together until foamy. Stir in the butter, then one after the other stir the flour, cocoa powder, raisins, cinnamon and cloves into the mixture.

3 Whisk the egg whites until stiff and carefully fold into the batter. Turn the batter into the prepared loaf pan and smooth the top.

4 Bake in the oven for about 1 hour. Leave to cool slightly in the pan, and then remove from the pan and leave to cool completely.

5 To serve, whisk the cream with vanilla extract until stiff. Spread on top of the cake and sprinkle with cinnamon.

Serves about 12

BLUEBERRY MUFFINS

Ingredients

¼ cup/50 g butter

1 egg

3 tbsp. honey

Scant ½ cup/100 ml plain yogurt

Scant ½ cup/100 ml sour cream

2½ cups/250 g all-purpose
(plain) flour

2 tsp. baking powder

2½ cups/250 g blueberries

Confectioners' (icing) sugar, for dusting

Method

Prep and cook time: 40 min.

1 Preheat the oven to 180°C/350°F/Gas Mark 4.
Line a 12 hole muffin pan with paper cases. Melt
the butter and leave to cool slightly, so that it is still
liquid.

2 Put the egg, honey, yogurt and sour cream in
a large bowl and mix together. Stir in the melted
butter. Sift in the flour and baking powder and mix
together. Fold in the blueberries. Fill the muffin pan
three-quarters full with the batter.

3 Bake in the oven for 25-30 minutes, until golden
brown. Leave to rest in the pan for 5 minutes, and
then remove from the pan and leave to cool on a
wire rack. Serve dusted with confectioners'
(icing) sugar.

Makes 12

APPLE CRUMBLE CAKE

Ingredients

½ cup/125 g butter, plus extra
for greasing

⅔ cup/125 g sugar

3 eggs

1 tsp vanilla extract

½ cup/125 g quark or low-fat
cream cheese

3 tbsp. cornstarch (cornflour)

1½ tsp. baking powder

2 cups/200 g all-purpose (plain) flour

1 lb 6 oz/600 g apples

For the crumble

⅓ cup/75 g butter

⅔ cup/75 g all-purpose (plain) flour

Scant 1 cup/75 g ground almonds

2 tbsp. sugar

1 tsp. cinnamon

Method

Prep and cook time: 1 hour 15 min.

1 Preheat the oven to 180°C/350°F/Gas
Mark 4. Butter a 10 inch/26 cm spring-release
cake pan (tin).

2 Beat the butter and sugar together until light
and fluffy. Beat in the eggs, one at a time, and then
add the vanilla extract and the quark or cream
cheese and mix well together. Sift in the cornstarch
(cornflour), baking powder and flour and stir into
the mixture.

3 Peel, quarter, core and chop the apples and fold
into the batter. Turn the batter into the prepared
cake pan.

4 To make the crumble, melt the butter. Mix
the flour, ground almonds, sugar and cinnamon
together and add the melted the butter. Mix to a
crumbly mixture and scatter on top of the cake.

5 Bake in the oven for 40-50 minutes, until golden
brown. Leave to cool in the tin before serving.

Serves about 12

CHERRY CAKE WITH ALMOND CRUMBLE

Ingredients

¼ cup/50 g butter, plus extra for greasing

¾ oz/20 g fresh yeast

Scant ½ cup/100 ml lukewarm milk

2½ cups/250 g all-purpose (plain) flour, plus extra for dusting

2 tbsp. sugar

For the filling:

2¼ lb/1 kg cherries (from a jar)

4 eggs

Pinch of salt

¾ cup/150 g sugar

2/3 cup/150 g soft butter

1 cup/250 g cream cheese

4 tsp. almond liqueur

1¾ cups/150 g ground almonds

For the crumble:

1⅓ cups/150 g all-purpose (plain) flour

1⅓ cups/100 g flaked almonds

¾ cup/150 g sugar

2/3 cup/150 g butter

Method

Prep and cook time: 2 hours

1 Melt the butter. Cream the yeast smoothly with the milk. Put the flour, sugar and butter into a large bowl, add the yeast mixture and knead to a smooth dough. Cover and leave to rise in a warm place for 45 minutes.

2 Preheat the oven to 180°C/350°F/Gas Mark 4. Butter an 8x12 inch/20x30 cm baking pan (tin). To make the filling, drain the cherries. Separate the eggs. Whisk the egg whites with the salt until stiff, trickling in half of the sugar. Put the butter, remaining sugar, egg yolks, cream cheese and liqueur in a large bowl and beat together until light and fluffy. Stir in the ground almonds and lightly fold in the whisked egg whites.

3 Knead the dough on a floured work surface. Roll out thinly and use to line the prepared baking pan (tin). forming a raised rim around the edge. Spread the filling smoothly on the dough and scatter with the cherries.

4 To make the crumble, put the flour, flaked almonds, butter, in small pieces, in a bowl and mix together with your fingers to form a crumbly mixture. Add the sugar to the mix. Scatter the crumble on top of the cake. Bake in the oven for 40–45 minutes until golden brown.

Makes 16

CHOCOLATE SHEET CAKE

Ingredients

5 oz/150 g dark chocolate (70% cocoa solids)

Scant 1 cup/200 g soft butter

1 cup/150 g confectioners' (icing) sugar

8 eggs

½ cup/100 g sugar

1½ cups/150 g all-purpose (plain) flour

⅓ cup/50 g unsalted peanuts, finely ground

4 tbsp. cocoa powder

For the frosting:

¼ cup/50 ml whipping cream

7 oz/200 g dark chocolate (70% cocoa solids)

½ cup/75 g unsalted peanuts, roughly chopped

Method

Prep and cook time: 1 hour 15 min.

1 Preheat the oven to 180°C/350°F/Gas Mark 4. Line an 8 x 12 inch/20x30 cm baking pan (tin) with baking parchment. Break the chocolate into a bowl and melt over a saucepan of simmering water. Remove from the heat and allow to cool.

2 Put the butter and confectioners' (icing) sugar in a bowl and beat together until light and fluffy. Separate the eggs and gradually beat the egg yolks and the melted chocolate into the creamed butter.

3 Whisk the egg whites and sugar together until stiff. Carefully fold into the chocolate mixture. Mix the flour, ground peanuts and cocoa together and fold into the mixture. Spread the batter in the prepared baking pan.

4 Bake in the oven for 35-40 minutes, until a wooden cocktail stick inserted into the middle comes out clean. Leave to cool.

5 To make the frosting, warm the cream in a pan. Break in the chocolate and stir until melted. Leave to cool slightly then spread on top of the cake. Scatter over the peanuts and cut into pieces. Leave to cool completely before serving.

Makes about 24

MISSISSIPPI MUD CAKE

Ingredients

1 cup/250 g butter, plus extra for greasing

Cocoa powder

1¼ cups/300 ml strong coffee

¼ cup/60 ml whiskey

5½ oz/150 g dark chocolate (at least 30% cocoa solids)

2 cups/375 g sugar

2½ cups/250 g all-purpose (plain) flour

1 tsp. baking powder

1 tsp. baking soda

Pinch of salt

1 vanilla bean (pod)

2 eggs

Confectioners' (icing) sugar, for dusting

Whipped cream, to serve

Method

Prep and cook time 2 hours

1 Preheat the oven to 120°C/250°F/Gas Mark ½. Butter a large ring cake pan (tin), measuring about 11 inch/28 cm, and dust with cocoa powder.

2 Put the coffee and whiskey in a saucepan and heat slowly. Break in the chocolate, add the butter in small pieces, and stir constantly until melted and smooth. Remove from the heat, stir in the sugar and leave to cool slightly.

3 Transfer the mixture to a large bowl and, using a hand-held electric whisk, gradually mix in the flour, baking powder, baking soda and salt at a low speed. Split and scrape out the seeds from the vanilla bean (pod) and add to the mixture. Add the eggs and mix until smooth. Pour the batter into the prepared cake pan.

4 Bake in the oven for 90–100 minutes, until a wooden cocktail stick inserted into the middle comes out clean. Leave to cool slightly, and then carefully turn out on to a wire rack. Dust with confectioners' (icing) sugar and serve with whipped cream.

Serves 10-12

LEMON GINGER CAKE

Ingredients

1⅓ cups/300 g soft butter, plus extra for greasing

1½ cups/150 g all-purpose (plain) flour, plus extra for dusting

1⅓ cups/250 g sugar

5 eggs

1 cup/150 g cornstarch (cornflour)

2 tsp. freshly grated ginger

Zest of 2 unwaxed lemons

For the syrup:

Zest of 1 unwaxed lemon

Scant ½ cup/100 ml lemon juice

3 tbsp. confectioners' (icing) sugar

Method

Prep and cook time: 1 hour 30 min.

1 Preheat the oven to 180°C/350°F/Gas Mark 4. Butter a 6 cup/1.5 litre loaf pan (tin) and dust with flour.

2 Put the butter and two-thirds of the sugar in a large bowl and beat together until light and fluffy. Separate the eggs and beat the egg yolks into the creamed mixture. Add the flour, cornstarch (cornflour), ginger and half the lemon zest and quickly combine.

3 Whisk the egg whites with the remaining sugar until stiff. Stir a little into the batter and then carefully fold in the rest. Turn the batter into the prepared loaf pan and smooth the top.

4 Bake in the oven for about 1 hour, until a wooden cocktail stick inserted into the middle comes out clean.

5 Meanwhile, make the glaze. Put the lemon zest, juice and confectioners' (icing) sugar in a saucepan and simmer until reduced to a syrupy consistency. When the cake is cooked, sprinkle with the lemon syrup. Leave to cool slightly in the loaf pan and then transfer to a wire rack. Scatter the remaining lemon zest on top and leave to cool completely.

Serves 8–10

CHERRY CAKE

Ingredients

1/3 cup/90 g butter, plus extra for greasing

3 cups/750 g cherries

1/2 cup/90 g sugar

2 large eggs

3/4 cup/75 g all-purpose (plain) flour

1 tsp. baking powder

1/2 cup/50 g ground almonds

Confectioners' (icing) sugar, for dusting

Method

Prep and cook time: 1 hour

1 Preheat the oven to 200°C/400°F/Gas Mark 6. Butter an 8 1/2 inch/22 cm spring-release cake pan (tin) and line the base with baking parchment.

2 Remove the pits (stones) from the cherries. Put the butter and sugar in a large bowl and beat together until thick and creamy. Gradually beat in the eggs and stir in the flour with the baking powder and ground almonds.

3 Mix half the cherries into the batter. Turn the batter into the prepared cake pan and put the remaining cherries on top.

4 Bake in the oven for about 40-50 minutes. Remove from the cake pan and leave to cool. Dust with confectioners' (icing) sugar before serving.

Serves 8

COFFEE ROULADE

Ingredients

4 eggs plus 2 egg yolks

Pinch of salt

1/3 cup/60 g sugar

1 tsp. vanilla extract

1¼ cups/125 g all-purpose (plain) flour

½ tsp. baking powder

Sugar, for sprinkling

For the filling

2/3 cup/150 g spoonable heavy (double) cream

1 cup/250 g mascarpone cheese

½ oz/15 g cocoa powder

3 tbsp. instant coffee powder

½ cup/100 g sugar

1 cup/250 ml whipping cream

Chocolate-coated coffee beans, for decoration

2 tbsp. cocoa powder, for dusting

Method

Prep and cook time 45 min. plus 3 hours cooling and chilling

1 Preheat the oven to 200°C/400°F/Gas Mark 6. Line a baking pan (tin), measuring about 15 x 10x ¾ inch /38 x 25 x 2cm, with parchment paper.

2 To make the sponge, separate the eggs. Whisk the egg whites and salt together until stiff. Put the egg yolks, sugar and vanilla extract into a large bowl and beat together until foamy. Sift in the flour and baking powder and stir into the mixture. Fold in the whisked egg whites. Spread the batter smoothly into the prepared baking pan.

3 Bake in the oven for 8-10 minutes. Turn out on to a tea towel sprinkled with sugar. Pull off the baking parchment and roll the sponge up with the tea towel. Leave to cool.

4 For the filling, put the spoonable cream, mascarpone cheese, cocoa powder, instant coffee powder and sugar in a large bowl and stir together until the coffee has dissolved. Whisk the whipping cream until stiff and fold about four-fifths into the mixture.

5 Spread the coffee cream on the sponge and roll up. Chill well before serving. Dust with cocoa powder and decorate with the reserved cream piped on top and the chocolate-coated coffee beans.

Serves 8

COCONUT CHOCOLATE CAKE

Ingredients

6 eggs

Scant 1 cup/180 g sugar

1 cup/100 g all-purpose (plain) flour

1½ tsp. baking powder

1⅓ cups/100 g grated coconut

For the filling:

⅔ cup/50 g toasted grated coconut

1½ tbsp. cornstarch (cornflour)

2 tbsp. cocoa powder

1 cup/225 ml milk

½ tsp. vanilla extract

1 tbsp. sugar

3½ oz/100 g chocolate spread

For the decoration:

⅔ cup/200 g apricot conserve

1⅓ cups/100 g grated coconut

Chocolate curls

Red currants

Method

Prep and cook time: 1 hour 30 min.

1 Preheat the oven to 180°C/350°F/Gas Mark 4. Grease a 10 inch/26 cm spring- release cake pan (tin) and line with baking parchment.

2 To make the cake, separate the eggs. Whisk the egg whites with the sugar until stiff. Stir in the egg yolks. Sift in the flour and baking powder and fold into the mixture with the grated coconut. Turn the batter into the prepared cake pan and smooth the top.

3 Bake in the oven for about 40 minutes. Leave to cool slightly, and then remove from the cake pan and leave cool completely.

4 Meanwhile, make the filling. Briefly toast the grated coconut in a non-stick skillet (frying pan) until lightly browned. Mix the cornstarch (cornflour) and cocoa powder with a little of the milk. Pour the remaining milk into a saucepan and gently heat. Add the cornstarch mixture, vanilla extract and sugar and bring to the boil, stirring all the time. Add the chocolate spread and sprinkle the surface with the toasted coconut. Leave to cool.

5 To decorate, split the cake horizontally. Put the bottom half of the cake on a serving plate. Stir the filling mixture and spread on to the cake half. Place the top half of the cake on top.

6 Warm the apricot conserve and spread all over the surface of the cake. Sprinkle the cake on all sides with grated coconut and decorate with chocolate curls and red currants.

Serves 8

CHOCOLATE COFFEE SLICE

Ingredients

7 oz/200 g dark chocolate
(60-70% cocoa solids)

3½ oz/100 g coffee flavored
chocolate (40-50% cocoa solids)

6 eggs

Pinch of salt

1½ cups/300 g sugar

4 tsp. strong espresso coffee

1 1/3 cups/300 g margarine

1½ cups/150 g all-purpose (plain)
flour

For the topping:

½ cup/70 g cornstarch (cornflour)

½ cup/100 g sugar

3 1/3 cups/800 ml milk

1 vanilla bean (pod)

Scant 1 cup/200 g butter

For the fruit compote:

1 ripe mango

½ papaya

Grated zest and juice 2 limes

Sugar, to taste

Method

Prep and cook time: 1 hour 30 min. plus 5 hours chilling time

1 Preheat the oven to 180°C/350°F/Gas Mark 4. Grease a baking pan (tin), preferably with loose-sides, measuring about 13x9 in/35x24 cm and dust with flour.

2 Break the chocolate into a bowl and melt over a saucepan of simmering water. Separate the eggs. Beat the egg yolks, sugar and espresso coffee together until thick and foamy and the sugar has dissolved. Whisk the egg whites and salt together until stiff.

3 Remove the chocolate from the heat and stir in the margarine, a few small pieces at a time. Fold into the egg yolk mixture. Sift in the flour and fold in with the whisked egg whites. Turn the batter into the prepared baking pan. Bake in the oven for 25-30 minutes.

4 Meanwhile, mix the cornstarch (cornflour) and sugar with a little of the milk until smooth. Slit open the vanilla bean (pod) and scrape out the seeds. Put the remaining milk in a saucepan with the vanilla bean and seeds and bring to a boil. As soon as the milk boils remove the pan from the heat and stir in the cornstarch mixture. Return to the boil briefly, stirring constantly. Remove from the heat, take out the vanilla bean and let cool slightly, stirring. Gradually stir in the butter.

5 When the cake is cooked, leave to cool slightly and then turn out on to a board. Put the sides of the baking pan around the cake and spread the vanilla cream smoothly on top. Chill in the refrigerator for at least 5 hours.

6 Peel the mango, cut the flesh away from the pit (stone) and dice the flesh. Peel the papaya, remove the seeds and dice the flesh. Put the fruit, grated zest and lime juice in a pan and simmer for about 5 minutes. Sweeten to taste. Leave to cool.

7 To serve, cut the cake into pieces and serve decorated with a little fruit compote.

Makes 12

CHOCOLATE BANANA LOAF

Ingredients

6 eggs

1¾ cups/350 g sugar

3 large bananas

3 tsp. vanilla extract

1 cup/250 ml advocaat

1¼ cups/300 ml sunflower oil

2 cups/200 g all-purpose (plain) flour

1¹⁄₃ cups/200 g cornstarch (cornflour)

3 tsp. baking powder

½ cup/100 g chocolate chips

Confectioners' (icing) sugar or
chocolate frosting, to decorate
(optional)

Method

Prep and cook time 2 hours

1 Preheat the oven to 180°C/350°F/Gas Mark 4.
Grease a 12 inch/30 cm loaf pan (tin).

2 Put the eggs and sugar in a large bowl and beat
together until thick and foamy. Mash the bananas
and stir into the egg mixture with the vanilla extract
and advocaat. Add the oil and stir in the flour,
cornstarch (cornflour), baking powder and chocolate
chips. Turn the mixture into the prepared loaf pan.

3 Bake in the oven for about 80 minutes, until
a wooden cocktail stick inserted into the middle
comes out clean. Cover with foil for the last 30
minutes. Leave to cool and serve dusted with
confectioners' (icing) sugar or drizzled with
chocolate frosting, if you wish.

Serves about 12

GINGERBREAD BUNDT CAKE

Ingredients

1 cup/250 g soft butter

1¹/₃ cups/250 g sugar

5 eggs

5 cups/500 g all-purpose (plain) flour

½ tsp salt

3 tsp. baking powder

2 tsp. gingerbread, apple pie or mixed spice

3 tbsp. cocoa powder

1 cup/250 ml milk

2 tbsp. cream cheese

5 tbsp. whipping cream

5 tbsp. confectioners' (icing) sugar

Method

Prep and cook time: 1 hour 30 min. plus 2 hours chilling

1 Preheat the oven to 325°F/ 170°C/Gas Mark 3. Grease a bundt cake mold (mould).

2 Put the butter and sugar in a large bowl and beat together until light and fluffy. Add the eggs and beat until pale and creamy. Sift in the flour, salt, baking powder, spice and cocoa powder and stir into the mixture. Gradually stir in enough milk to produce a soft batter. Turn the batter into the prepared cake mold.

3 Bake in the oven for about 1 hour, until a wooden cocktail stick inserted into the middle comes out clean. Cover with foil if it browns too quickly. Turn out on to a wire rack and leave to cool.

4 To make the frosting, put the cream cheese and cream in a large bowl and mix together. Add the confectioners' (icing) sugar and mix well. Drizzle the frosting over the cold cake and chill for 1-2 hours before serving.

Serves about 8

WALNUT COFFEE CAKE

Ingredients

1 vanilla bean (pod)

1 cup/250 g soft butter

4 eggs

2/3 cup/220 g dark and aromatic honey

2 cups/ 200 g all-purpose (plain) flour

3 tsp. baking powder

1 tsp. cinnamon

2 1/3 cups/200 g finely ground walnuts

Scant ½ cup/100 ml cream sherry

For the filling and decoration:

7 oz/200 g white chocolate

Scant ½ cup/100 ml whipping cream

2 tsp. instant coffee espresso powder

3–4 tbsp. walnut liqueur, optional

8 small chocolate eggs

A few walnut halves

Method

Prep and cook time: 1 hour 45 min. plus 4 hours cooling

1 Preheat the oven to 180°C/350°F/Gas Mark 4. Line a 9 in/24 cm spring-release cake pan (tin) with parchment paper.

2 Slit open the vanilla bean (pod) and scrape out the seeds. Beat the butter in a large bowl and gradually beat in the eggs, honey and vanilla seeds. Sift in the flour, baking powder and cinnamon, add the ground walnuts and stir into the mixture. Stir in the sherry. Turn the batter into the prepared cake pan.

3 Bake in the oven for about 1 hour, until a wooden cocktail stick inserted into the middle comes out clean. Cover with foil if the cake darkens too quickly. Leave to cool slightly, and then turn out on to a wire rack and let cool completely.

4 To make the filling, chop the chocolate and put in a bowl. Put the cream in a saucepan, add the espresso powder, let it dissolve then bring to a boil. Pour on to the chocolate and stir until the chocolate has melted. Stir in the liqueur (if using), leave to cool slightly, and then beat briefly with a hand-held electric whisk.

5 Split the cake horizontally and spread the bottom layer with half of the cream filling. Replace the top layer and spread the remaining cream on top of the cake. Decorate with chocolate eggs and walnuts and leave the cream to set before serving.

Serves 6-8

PEANUT BUTTER AND JELLY BARS

Ingredients

²/₃ cup/100 g peanuts

2 cups/200 g all-purpose (plain) flour

Scant ½ cup/100 g butter

½ cup/100 g peanut butter

1 egg

¾ cup/100 g confectioners' (icing) sugar

1 tsp. salt

¾ cup /250 g strawberry conserve

1 egg yolk

Method

Prep and cook time: 1 hour 30 min. plus 1 hour chilling

1 Finely crush the peanuts with a pestle and mortar. Put the flour, butter, peanut butter and peanuts in a large bowl. Add the egg, confectioners' (icing) sugar and salt and mix to a smooth dough. Wrap in plastic wrap (clingfilm) and chill in the refrigerator for 1 hour.

2 Preheat the oven to 180°C/350°F/Gas Mark 4. Press half of the dough into a square 8 inch/20 cm baking pan (tin), preferably with loose-sides, and spread with the strawberry conserve to within ½ inch/1 cm of the edge.

3 Roll out the remaining dough to fit the baking pan and lay on top of the filling. Press the edges together well. Whisk the egg yolk with a dash of water and use to glaze the top of the cake.

4 Bake in the oven for about 50 minutes. Remove from the pan and leave to cool. Cut into bars to serve.

Makes about 6

CHOCOLATE LAYER CAKE

Ingredients

6 eggs

1 cup/180 g sugar

1 tsp. vanilla extract

Scant 1¼ cups/120 g flour

½ cup/80 g cornstarch (cornflour)

For the filling and frosting:

3 tbsp. cornstarch (cornflour)

3 tbsp. cocoa powder

2 tbsp. sugar

2 cups/500 ml milk

5 oz/150 g Gianduja (chocolate and hazelnut flavored chocolate)

1⅓ cups/300 g butter

Method

Prep and cook time: 1 hour 15 min. plus 2–3 h resting time

1 Preheat the oven to 180°C/350°F/Gas Mark 4. Grease the base of an 8½ inch/22 cm spring-release cake pan (tin) and wrap a piece of folded, greased baking parchment around the outside to increase the height of the pan by about a third.

2 Separate the eggs. Beat the egg yolks with half of the sugar and the vanilla extract until foamy. Sift the flour and cornstarch over the mixture and fold in.

3 Whisk the egg whites until they form soft peaks, then trickle in the remaining sugar and continue whisking until they form stiff peaks. Fold the whisked egg whites into the egg yolk mixture. Turn the batter into the prepared cake pan and smooth the top.

4 Bake in the oven for 25–30 minutes, until a wooden cocktail stick inserted into the middle comes out clean. Leave to cool slightly, then carefully turn out on to a wire rack and let the cake rest for at least 2 hours.

5 When ready to fill, make the frosting. Put the cornstarch, cocoa powder and sugar in a bowl and mix together with a little cold milk until smooth. Put the remaining milk in a saucepan, bring to a boil and stir in the cornstarch mixture. Return to a boil briefly, then remove from heat. Break in the Gianduja and stir until the chocolate is completely melted and the mixture is smooth. Finally, stir in the butter, one tablespoon at a time, and then allow to cool.

6 Split the cake twice horizontally. Spread half of the frosting smoothly over the two lower layers of cake. Reassemble the cake with the third (unfrosted) layer on top. Spread the top and sides of the cake with the remaining cream. Chill until ready to serve.

Serves 8

LEMON BARS

Ingredients

2½ cups/250 g all-purpose (plain) flour, plus extra for dusting

1 tsp. baking powder

Scant ½ cup/100 g cold butter

1/3 cup/75 g sugar

1 egg

For the filling

6 tbsp. cornstarch (cornflour)

2 tsp. vanilla extract

8 tbsp. sugar

3 1/3 cups/800 ml milk

4 eggs

Grated zest of 1 lemon

Large pinch of saffron

1 cup/150 g confectioners' (icing) sugar

Method

Prep and cook time: 1 hour 30 min. plus at least 4 hours chilling time

1 To make the pastry, sift the flour and baking powder into a bowl. Add the butter in small pieces, the sugar and egg, and quickly work into the flour to form a dough. Wrap the dough in plastic wrap (clingfilm) and chill in the refrigerator for 30 minutes.

2 To make filling, mix the cornstarch (cornflour), vanilla extract and sugar with a little of the milk until smooth. Pour the remaining milk into a saucepan, bring to the boil and then stir in the cornstarch mixture. Return to the boil, stirring all the time. Leave to cool slightly.

3 Preheat the oven to 180°C/350°F/Gas Mark 4. Roll out the pastry on a floured work surface and use to line a 15 x 10 x ¾ inch/38 x 25 x 2 cm baking pan (tin). Prick several times with a fork.

4 Bake in the oven for about 10 minutes. Meanwhile, separate the eggs. Stir the egg yolks into the filling mixture with the lemon zest and saffron. Whisk the egg whites until stiff and fold into the mixture.

5 Spread the lemon filling on the pastry and bake in the oven for a further 30-40 minutes. Leave to cool completely, preferably overnight.

6 Before serving, dust thickly with confectioners' (icing) sugar and cut into pieces.

Makes 30

PEACH ALMOND TART

Ingredients

2 cups/200 g all-purpose (plain) flour

Scant ½ cup/100 g cold butter

Pinch of salt

1–2 tbsp. cold water

For the filling:

3 eggs

¾ cup/150 g sugar

²/₃ cup 150 g spoonable heavy (double) cream

2 tbsp. lemon juice

1 tsp. lemon zest

¹/₃ cup/75 g butter

1¾ cups/150 g ground almonds

3–4 peaches, depending on size

Method

Prep and cook time: 1h 25 min. plus 1 h resting

1 Put the flour, butter in small pieces, and salt in a large bowl and rub in with your fingers to make a crumbly mixture. Add the water to make a dough. Form into a ball, wrap in plastic wrap (clingfilm) and put into the refrigerator for about 1 hour.

2 Preheat the oven to 180°C/350°F/Gas Mark 4. Roll out the pastry on a floured work surface and use to line a 9–10 inch/24-26 cm tart pan (tin). Cut off the excess by rolling over the top of the pan with your rolling pin. Line with a sheet of baking parchment and weigh down with dried beans. Bake in the oven for 20 minutes. Remove the baking parchment and dried beans.

3 Meanwhile, put the eggs and sugar in a bowl and beat together until thick and foamy. Stir in the cream, lemon juice and lemon zest and add the butter in small pieces. Stand the bowl over a saucepan of simmering water and beat with an electric whisk until thick and creamy. Stir in the ground almonds.

4 Drop the peaches into boiling water for a few seconds, then skin, halve, remove the pits (stones) and slice thinly.

5 Spread the almond filling smoothly into the hot pastry shell and arrange the peach slices attractively on top.

6 Bake in the oven for about 45 minutes, until the filling is set. It should be lightly browned, but cover with foil if it browns too quickly. Leave to cool before serving.

Serves 6-8

ORANGE POPPY SEED CAKE

Ingredients

¾ cup /180 g butter, plus extra for greasing

3 cups/300 g all-purpose (plain) flour

1½ tsp. baking powder

¾ cup/150 g sugar

4 eggs

About 3 tbsp. milk

1 tsp. orange zest

For the orange caramel

Scant 1 cup/100 ml water

1 cup/200 g sugar

¼ cup/50 g butter

3–4 unwaxed oranges

For the poppy seed mixture

Heaped ⅓ cup/50 g raisins

1 tbsp. rum

¼ cup/60 ml milk

2 tbsp./25 g soft butter

1 cup/125 g ground poppy seeds

2–4 tbsp sugar

Finely-chopped candied lemon or orange peel

1 egg, if necessary

Method

Prep and cook time: 2 hours

1 Grease an 11 inch/22 cm spring-release cake pan (tin). Put the raisins for the poppy seed mixture in a bowl, add the rum and leave to soak.

2 Meanwhile, make the caramel. Put the water and sugar in a saucepan and heat until brown and caramelized. Remove from the heat, stir in the butter and immediately pour into the cake tin, coating both the base and sides. Slice the oranges very thinly and press neatly on to the base and sides of the prepared cake pan, overlapping them slightly.

3 To make the poppy seed mixture, pour the milk into a saucepan, add the butter and bring to the boil. Stir in the poppy seeds, sugar to taste, and add the candied lemon or orange peel and the raisins. Set aside and leave to cool. When cold, stir in the egg, if necessary, to bind the mixture together.

4 Preheat the oven to 180°C/350°F/Gas Mark 4. To make the cake, put the butter, flour, baking powder, sugar, eggs, milk, orange zest, and the poppy seed mixture and into a large bowl and mix to a smooth batter. Stir in a little more milk if the batter is too stiff. Turn into the orange-lined cake pan and smooth the top.

5 Bake in the oven for 50-60 minutes, until a wooden cocktail stick inserted into the middle comes out clean. Leave to cool slightly then turn out on to a serving plate and leave to cool completely.

Serves about 10

Published by Transatlantic Press

First published in 2010

Transatlantic Press
38 Copthorne Road, Croxley Green, Hertfordshire WD3 4AQ

© Transatlantic Press

Images and Recipes by StockFood © The Food Image Agency

Recipes selected by Jonnie Léger, StockFood

A catalogue record for this book is available from the British Library.

ISBN 978-1-908533-52-4

Printed in China

HAZELNUT AND CHOCOLATE CAKE

Ingredients

1¾ cups/300 g hazelnuts

5 eggs

Scant ½ cup/100 g soft butter

1½ cups/300 g sugar

¾ cup/80 g cocoa powder

Confectioners' (icing) sugar, for dusting

Method

Prep and cook time: 1 hour 30 min.

1 Preheat the oven to 220°C/425°F/Gas Mark 7. Line the sides of a 9 in/24 cm spring-release cake pan (tin) with baking parchment.

2 Spread the hazelnuts out on a baking sheet and toast in the oven for 12-15 minutes. Put on a tea towel and rub off the skin. Put in a food processor and grind the nuts finely.

3 Reduce the oven temperature to 180°C/350°F/Gas Mark 4. Separate the eggs. Whisk the egg whites with ½ cup/100 g of the sugar until stiff. Beat the egg yolks with the remaining sugar until creamy. Add the butter a few small pieces at a time and beat until the mixture is very thick and creamy.

4 Mix the ground nuts with the cocoa powder and fold into the egg yolk mixture. Fold in the whisked egg whites. Turn the batter into the prepared cake pan.

5 Bake in the oven for 45-50 minutes, until a wooden cocktail stick inserted into the middle comes out clean. Leave to cool slightly then remove from the cake pan and leave to cool completely. Serve dusted generously with confectioners' (icing) sugar.

Serves 8-10